# Win Today

## A Jersey Girl's Guide to **Living Your Best Life!**

### MARY ELLEN LORANGER

# Contents

## Section 1

### Jersey Girl Says What to Start Doing

# Section 2
## What Jersey Girl Says to Stop Doing

# *Introduction*

Funerals are usually dark, sad, and dreary. But not this one. This funeral was all about light, love, and transformation. A weight was lifted off my shoulders and a re-birth was witnessed internally and externally.

I could feel my old self seeping away and my new self-becoming whole. As if I was shedding dead skin and growing wings like a butterfly. **This was a funeral of self. A funeral I was witnessing where I had a front-row seat to say goodbye to the old me and hello to the new.**

Days prior to this little self-given mental funeral, I was not where I wanted to be in life. It was around age 40, quite possibly an early midlife crisis, when I started hearing this whisper: *Is this it? Is this all there is?* I felt stuck. Too comfortable. Uneasy and restless. Those whispers got louder, would speak to me often, and then became a deafening roar. So I decided.

**I was meant for more.**

This funeral I gave to myself was an agreement to myself to be the best version of me. I needed to create my best life yet, with no regrets and no excuses. A winning life.

So, what if today you decided you're sick of playing from the sidelines too?

Sick of getting in your own damn way! Sick of always being afraid? And most importantly, sick of putting your dreams on the back burner. What if today was the day you decided to be reborn and decided to win?

I don't think anyone is necessarily born to win. But it is something you have to develop, polish, fine-tune and work very hard at and it will work back in your favor. Like a muscle you develop by lifting weights. Winning is a belief you have to build up over time; based on past experiences, failures, and more failures, trying and trying again.

On one sunny day out on the Jersey Shore when I was a ten-year-old little girl in the 1970s, I was riding on one of those rubber rafts on the edge of the ocean with my mom. I was scared. She said to me, "Just let these tiny waves take you out to the small waves. Then to the bigger waves. See how you feel about that first."

And I did that for a while, but then I saw my brother and dad out farther in the huge waves and I wanted to be out there too. I wanted to be where the big action was, but I couldn't get there until I mastered my fear of the tiny waves first. So I will equate these waves to wins.

*To win big you have to start small.*

Let's start by achieving some small wins first.

Let that momentum build like the waves then. It creates confidence and increases your bravery bone, if you will, so you can rise to the bigger waves and go on to attempt the bigger wins in your life and **ride the winning wave!**

Girl, no matter where you've been or what you are dealing with now, you were meant to do something pretty special with your life. Knowing this helps you to start convincing your unconscious belief system and your conscious self that you deserve more—a happy life, to follow your dreams, and to create a new you.

When we feel we are accomplished in something, when we feel we are winning, when we start the day winning, we're building up those deposits in the *"Bank of You"*. And the Bank of You is a belief in yourself. A belief is something you know is absolute truth, without a shadow of a doubt. It helps shape our current reality and determines our success.

Because when you believe something is possible for yourself, you get your mind wired to win. That's why it's so important to get your "belief bank" full up as we set out on this journey together. So the next time you try to convince yourself you deserve more, you can pull from this Bank of You. Our goal is to build up those beliefs that support the new you and let go of the ones that don't.

We will also learn how to create and check off our "Winning Wowzas" each day—not a to-do list per se—but a checklist of small wins that make huge differences. These will help you stay accountable, build momentum and propel you forward. When we stay true to our commitments and get back to it each day, even on the days we don't feel like it, even when we are uncomfortable, we increase our grit factor which contributes to weaving in a winning mentality.

If you're looking for this winning checklist, you can go to www.wintodaybook.com to snag yours.

If an egg breaks on the inside, life begins. When it breaks on the outside, life ends. When you want to move forward, it's not external factors that stop you. It's internal stuff going on inside that holds you back. This is why it is imperative that you get your Bank of You and your "Wowzas" in check because these will help with your internal wins.

You have something magical inside you. You do have what it takes to be all you were meant to be. But it's your thoughts, negative self-talk, your attachment to your past, your failures, and setbacks you can't let go of. That victim mentality is robbing you of your greatness.

Winning will not happen overnight. Although we wish it could, nothing that is worth fighting for will ever magically happen with the snap of our fingers.

# How Can I Use This Book?

**O**ver the past several years, I've had the absolute privilege of transforming thousands of lives—in body, mind, spirit, and finances. Because I have helped others create meaningful change in their lives, I KNOW that living your BEST life *is* possible. That you have everything you need at this very moment to do what it takes to achieve your goals and follow your dreams. Your potential is unlimited. The fact that you are reading these words tells me you are open and ready for it...so I ask your permission today to **nudge** that potential and unlock the greatness inside of you!

However, it all begins with looking inside ourselves...and believing that WE CAN WIN. Because nothing can come to fruition unless it exists in our minds *first*.

Through this book, you will begin to think of growing as accumulative—when every day goes up *just* a notch from the day before. It's when you are consistent with the small steps, until you look back one day and can't believe how high up you are! We are on our way to creating a winning mindset.

What we do every day matters more than what we do once in a while. We will first focus on daily actions, not outcomes. Because if all of a sudden you're putting all of your hard work and focus into the actions, but you don't see results right away through the outcomes, you will get discouraged. But trust me, friend, the magic is happening, even if you don't see it at first. This is why we focus on *action, action, action*.

These small steps, done day in and day out, will become habits. They will free you up from decisions you make every day; whether or not you should be doing the things you know you need to do to move you forward in your life. In short, we will start by winning one day at a time.

It's like the coin analogy. If ten coins are not enough to make a man rich, what if you add one coin? What if you add another? Even though one coin isn't sufficient enough to make a man rich, a man only becomes rich by adding one coin after another, to stack them up. Like our actions, any one instance of an action might not seem like much, yet the sum of those actions is very important.

The big wins grow by stacking one small win at a time. The mere act of adding one coin to the heap at a time or stacking one small win at a time strengthens your winning streak and your belief in yourself.

**I want you to choose you. You are your best investment. Decide today that you are going to put in the work and show up for yourself.**

In this book, I want to walk you through how I got to where I am today in hopes of inspiring you to make simple changes in your own unique lives.

And once you make that decision, we begin now. So here we go, let this Jersey girl guide you. *I got you girlfriend!*

You're holding onto a winning blueprint that will keep you grounded and will help you take control of each day. When it becomes second nature and you feel more accomplished, the wave of winning builds more momentum and strengthens and then starts crashing and spilling over into all areas of your life. Before you know it, you are riding that winning wave each and every day *to become the best you yet.*

Now I want you to ask yourself two questions…

*What do I need to start doing?*
*What do I need to stop doing?*

**We will start to become aware of what we need to stop doing and start doing to win today and win at life!**

# Section 1

## Jersey Girl Says
## What to Start Doing

*Chapter 1*

## Give Yourself
## Permission to Shift

Sometimes the smallest step in the right direction ends up being the biggest step of all.

If you just take one step forward and win one day then the next, these will stack up to be major victories. The next thing you will realize is that you will be winning weeks, then months, then years. This philosophy creates a winning life.

It's time to step up from the sidelines and onto the field to play the game.

**You're ready.** You're so ready! You're capable. And you're unstoppable, really you are!

Let your old tendencies dissipate. I want you to give your old self a funeral too. And hey, if funerals aren't your thing, then come up with something else. But it's time to let your old self go. No longer will you put up with other people's bullcrap. No longer will you put your needs last. And no longer will you play small.

You are here for a reason. You are here to play big and take up space. You were made for more. And I know you feel it deep down in your gut too. It's go-time! ***Go big or go home.***

It's a great thing when you realize you are on your way to becoming the person your past is pushing you to become. **Knock knock!** Here she is. Ready and able like never before. Welcome friend. I knew you were ready.

### Becoming Who You're Meant to Be

Society tries to push it's hidden agenda on us. Especially if you're a woman. They tell you you must meet McDreamy and have a certain number of kids before you're thirty. You must buy a house with a white picket fence complete with a family dog. They will tell you to have a fancy career, as long as it's stable, with a steady income with benefits, of course.

Society will tell you your hair should look a certain way, you should dress like Vogue, and have no waistline, but with curves. This time-clock expectation that society puts on us especially, can be excruciating.

It causes us to compare our lives to unrealistic standards.

**I want you to break free from the mold. Despite what society, your family, your friends, *or yourself* may think you should or shouldn't do, I am giving you the key to step through that doorway of the unknown and into your dreams.**

I was once a victim, like many, of societal demands too. I had *the* secure job. Good benefits. Kids by a certain age. *Check, check, and check.*

But around the age of 40, something kept nagging at me. "Mary Ellen...there is something *more*." I researched "early mid-life crisis". I took up running. I joined a new gym. I even attempted to learn Spanish. But that didn't quench the fire that was burning inside me. It didn't drown out the voices. And one day I woke up and decided I just didn't want to spend the rest of my life asking *"What if..."*

While holding down my job as a hospital administrator, in 2019 I started a side hustle where I helped people with their health. And in six months I quickly surpassed the income I was making at my six figure job. Even more intoxicating than the income was the feeling I had upon awakening each day: *helping others set my soul on fire.* I felt a passion and purpose I had never experienced. I started to use every white space of my day to work my emerging health coaching business: I woke up early, used my lunch hours to speak to potential clients, spent my commutes talking to coaches on my team, held Zoom calls after dinner and participated in every training I could on the weekends. And the business grew. And grew some more. Finally, I had reached a critical juncture as I was spending the majority of my day as a health coach, many times hiding in hospital bathrooms or spare offices to do health assessments or coach explore Zooms.

I recently came across an old journal I was using around this time, and it was obvious I was having an internal struggle about whether to stay or go. Here are some excerpts I had written trying to convince myself to stay:

> I am *close* to home…
> I like my *small* office…
> I have a *good* assistant…
> I work for a *nice* hospital…
> I make a *decent* salary…

*Wowza!* Talk about playing small, living on the sidelines and *being ok with being OK*. Mediocre Mary Ellen!

Thank goodness my words didn't silence that voice in my head that grew louder by the day.

So I made a small step, *a decision*. I was tired of doing what others expected of me. Tired of playing small. Tired of building someone else's dream. *I wanted to build my own*.

Nothing begins without a decision, friends. So I made one and then created a plan: I will give my 25-plus year employer my notice, grace them with my presence until year-end to not leave them in the lurch (it was July), and bank my income from health coaching all the while to build a nice cushion for myself.

*Ummmm… yeah not so much*. That plan only existed in my mind.

My faithful employer gave me two weeks to pack up my shit and hit the road. *Don't let the door hit you on the way out sister!*

Ohhhhh SNAP!! Now, I had to make my little side hustle work. Plan B became plan A literally OVERNIGHT.

This caused me to put my big girl panties on, ***to pivot and shift***. But let me tell you that this was the best thing that ever happened to me. Not only was the structural tension I needed to take my business to the next level, but to truly find my life's calling and step into who I was really meant to be.

*It happened for me and not to me.*

That day the old me was finally buried deep 6 feet underground and the new me began.

The best part is, I made the decision to move and pivot. To get out of the 9-5 trap. I now make more money than I ever did at my steady job and I have so much flexibility in my day. My passions and purpose are united and it feels incredible to get to be a blessing to other people. THIS RIGHT HERE is what I want for you too girl.

## Be a Master of Your Thoughts

"Whether you think you can, or think you can't...you're right." Henry Ford

To win the day, you have to be a master at your own thoughts. Your thoughts are who you become, so you better be sure that you fill your mind with positive thoughts. How do we do this? *Be one step ahead of your thoughts.*

If you feel a negative thought coming through your mind, pause for a few seconds, breathe into it and let it pass. Tell yourself, "This no longer serves me," and let it go. Negative thoughts are like pesky plot twists of a novel. Learn to flip the script and choose a new story to tell. Stand back as if you're taking an aerial perspective of your thoughts. You are witnessing what is taking place, but you're not getting involved this time.

**Let it pass through like a wave.**

The more positive thoughts we have, the better days we will see and have in our life.

Write yourself affirmations or reminders on your phone. Do it in notebooks or sticky notes, whichever you prefer.

Say them outloud and look at them often.

When you can, compliment others and spread positive words. Also, go as far as to write a letter to yourself. Remind yourself of all the things you've accomplished, all the things that you are, all the wins that you've created, all the goals you have achieved. Dig deep girl. *Yes, you do have so much to already be proud of!*

You will notice the more positivity that goes out, the more that will flow back in like the current.

Look in the mirror today and give yourself permission to shift, pivot and change.

*What negative thoughts hold you back?*
*How can you flip this script?*

## Chapter 2

## Wake Up Choosing to Win

Be the kind of woman that when your feet hit the floor in the morning, the devil says, "Oh crap...she's up!" Wake up choosing to win the day.

*Everything we do in life is a choice. Attitudes are a choice and choices can be changed.*

We are either choosing to go towards our goals, or are moving further away from them. What you're not changing in your life you're actually choosing.

What are you choosing upon waking? To win or to lose? To be positive or negative? To be hopeful or doubtful?

You decide!

## Morning Routine - Sunrise Self-Care!

When you spend the early hours caring for yourself, filling your bucket and energizing yourself, you are creating positive momentum before the sun even comes up.

Self care and structure in the morning is one of the most effective and simplest ways to set a winning wave in motion. Begin your day stressed, unfocused and unproductive and you will likely have a similar type day. Start it strong, however, and you will likely have a focused, productive and energetic day!

Create a morning routine, which I refer to as *"Sunrise Self Care"*—that sets the tone for the day and primes your mind and body to perform at a winning level. Once you set this structure in place it will become automatic and second nature.

## Sunrise Self Care Itinerary

Wake Early
Create a Winning Mantra to Set Intentions
Gratitude and Journaling
Personal Development
Meditation
Exercise & Fuel

Give Some Love
Get Organized

## Wake Early, Set Intentions

Start off by waking up earlier. *Yes, you heard me!* Whether it be 15 minutes to an hour, we have to carve out this time to set the day on its proper course. The early bird catches the worm and successful people don't wake to the sun. Taking control of your day begins by getting a jump on it.

Next, set your intention for the day. What do you want your day to look like? You are in control. To effectively do this, I like to say a morning mantra. Here are a couple of suggestions:

Let's win this thing!
Win Today Woman!
You GOT this girl!
Let's catch that winning wave!
Let's go get us some winning wowzas!

Say your mantra and intention out loud or write it down on a piece of paper or in a journal or notebook.

As you will see here, I am a *big* believer in writing your intentions, gratitudes, goals, dreams and the like versus typing them. There is something extremely powerful, magical and effective about putting your pen to paper.

## Gratitude

When we are grateful for all we have, more things to be grateful for will come to us. Every single morning, write down at least three things you're grateful for. Your gratitude list can be in your journal, on a sticky note, yellow notepad, whatever works for you.

Focusing on what you're grateful for will release a trigger of joy and will make you feel happier. Once you start focusing on writing these down, it will become easier to write more down over time. And, your brain will develop more neural connections to literally help you see more positivity in the world because you're choosing to focus on gratitude. Who doesn't want that?

Just this morning for an example, my husband and I had a small fight, *and I chose to feel unhappy.* Remember...everything is a *choice.* I don't know why women do this sometimes. I wanted to be upset. I wanted to stay in my little bubble and just be.

But because I've been practicing my morning routines for over two years now, I wrote down my gratitude right after our argument and there were about ten items that came to me. My husband was one of them.

I focused and reflected on all of the things he did for me, for our family, for our household. And for all the things he does to make my life easier. And my anger immediately dissipated.

I could no longer stay in my anger. And just like that our little rant was over. I'm telling you this stuff works like magic.

## Journaling

Have a journal nearby and journal first thing in the morning. Writing things down helps clear your mind, clarifies goals, priorities and intentions. It keeps us motivated, helps us identify emotions and feelings, encourages daily progress, enables a higher level of thinking and more focused action.

When you free write and allow any thoughts to come onto paper, you allow yourself to let your unconscious mind come and be seen. Your letting energy hit your paper. Journaling helps you make sense of all your thoughts and gets them into the physical realm.

## Personal Development

You'll also want to work on some form of personal development in your morning. Whether that means working through a new course, listening to a podcast or reading a book, like this one. Or even reading the Bible.

You want to have a few moments of uninterrupted time where you are growing and learning. This will trickle down and help you feel satisfied in other areas of your life as you work on improving and educating yourself.

For example, take that course on how to start an online business you've been dreaming about and read some books about it. Take the leap and just do it. This way you'll feel unstuck about it and it will make you feel more fulfilled.

## Meditation

After waking, while morning is still quiet, tap into a guided meditation to lessen anxiety and boost your feel good hormones. Meditation will make you feel more energized and focused throughout the day. A guided meditation will also help you unlock your unconscious mind and bring your deepest desires to the surface. There are so many wonderful free apps available to download.

## Fuel and Move

Hydrating and fueling well in the morning is essential to setting your day up for success. A key habit I've instilled is drinking 24 ounces of cold water before caffeine to really get my juices flowing and my mind sharp. Research shows that what we taste first in our day we crave the most, and that's why water is the first thing to touch my lips in the morning (sorry Hubs!) It's also beneficial to fuel properly within an hour upon waking a meal which contains a good balance of carbohydrates, protein and fats.

Next up is healthy movement. A reformed cardio junkie and exercise over-achiever, I now use exercise as a *celebration for what my body is and not a punishment for what it is not.* Whether it's yoga, pilates, strength training, a run or walk around the block, exercise should *feel good* and build us up, not break us down.

## Give The Love

Go find your husband, your kids, the dog and go tell them you love them. Give them a hug. Kiss and greet them with an enthusiastic "GOOD MORNING! How did you sleep?" Before we set out winning in our day, make sure you acknowledge and appreciate the ones who will support you on your new path.

## Get Organized & Set Your Schedule

Before you get started for the day, get organized. Make your bed, wash your face, tidy up those couch throw pillows, file papers away, clean up any clutter around spaces you spend the most time in, and pick up clothes lying around your floor, even if it's just placing them on your dresser before leaving for the day. These little morning tasks may not seem like a big deal, but it sets the tone and will lead to more productivity throughout the remainder of the day.

Next, open that calendar because if there is one "boss babe" besides you, *your calendar is it.* I was notorious for letting the day control me as opposed to me controlling the day. But in order to win each day, *we* have to set the course and take charge. Figure out what you need to get done, how much time each item will take, and *go time block for it.* Scheduling your day will free you of having to make too many decisions on how you will spend your time, as well as what to say yes to and more importantly, *what to say no to.* Setting your schedule and honoring that calendar will help you get clear on priorities, eliminate all unnecessary distractions, and let go of unimportant tasks while inspiring you to focus on the important ones. When you make the time to win each day, *win each day you will.*

## No Bad Days

Would you believe me if I told you I don't have any bad days? I may have a moment or two, but a whole day? Nope. No bad days over here. And you know why? Because my blueprint works!

We're creating new habits that are so strong, they'll become second nature. We're starting with Sunrise Self Care, building up the Bank of You and acknowledging our small wins. Bad days will start being scared of you and will start running away in the other direction. Kiss those bad days goodbye.

I wasn't always a positive person. In fact I used to dread getting out of bed in the morning and would mentally rush to get through every moment. I always imagined negative outcomes and envisioned the worst things that could happen. This was compounded by checking my phone first thing in the morning. I would respond to others and start my day in a reactive state rather than a receiving state. No wonder I was always stressed, frazzled, impatient and all-over-the-place. In short, *a hot mess.*

The solution? Checking in with *myself* first thing in the morning and giving myself all the love and self care I need. I want that for you too.

*So how are you going to create your Sunrise Self Care?*
*What steps are you going to implement first?*

## Chapter 3

# Act As If You've Already Won

L et your outside persuade your inside. My father often recalls a story for me of when I was a little girl in the playground. I was "leading" a team of pretend firefighters around the sandbox with the charge. *"Come on team let's put out the fire!!"* I guess the five-year-old me was acting like a leader before I actually was one.

Now, I'm not going to tell you to fake it until you make it because I don't believe in that. Instead, let's try something different. *Act as if. Act as if you are already a leader. Act as if you are already a CEO. Act as if you are already a runner. Act as if you are already at your ideal weight. Act as if you are in control of your day. Act as if you've already won.*

## What You Wear Does Matter

When we look the part, we also feel the part. So yes, dressing for success is an important way to let your outside persuade your inside. Yes, it may be tempting to show up in sweatpants and a t-shirt for Zoom calls all day, but that will leave you feeling zapped of energy and will cause you to miss opportunities.

I want your appearance to match your attitude. **Show up ready for action.**

It doesn't have to be a business suit. But put on your good jeans, the crisp pair from White House Black Market. You know... the ones that make you feel sexy? Take out that headband and blow out your hair. Throw on some big, fancy earrings.

During quarantine, due to COVID-19, my whole team challenged each other to show up looking our best for Zoom calls while wearing our favorite jeans all while staying home. This helped us stay on track with our nutrition, but more than anything, it made us feel good about ourselves. It kept us accountable and more importantly, it saved us from going down that rabbit hole of getting too *comfortable* with our appearance.

My father used to say to my siblings and me when growing up, "You can always be overdressed, but I never want to see you underdressed." I remember a time when my dad showed up to a youth sports game of mine. I was probably in the fifth grade and he was dressed in a leather jacket and a peddlers cap. He *always* looked the part and acted as if he was upper class, even when he wasn't. At the time, I remember feeling slightly embarrassed about the way he showed up.

All the other parents would come casual in jeans and t-shirts or sweatshirts. Not my dad, he wouldn't dare. Looking back now, I actually respect that. Even when he sold his family business and money got tight, he always showed up for himself and challenged us to do the same. "No ball caps at the dinner table," he would tell my brothers.

*Act as if...*

One of the greatest things my father ever taught me was to look like a million bucks and show up for yourself. I want this for you too. I want you to feel like a million bucks. Our minds can play tricks on us sometimes. When you get ready for the day by rolling out of bed in sweatpants and barely brushing your hair, your body will respond with low energy. Since I now work from home, the majority of my business is on Zoom and the phone. If I really wanted to, I could stay in my sweats with no bra all day, never shower or wear make-up. But then my energy would be off, I feel frumpy and my day follows suit.

Imagine the kind of ways your body will respond if you get out of bed the first time the alarm goes off, you wash your face, and you get dressed in colors that excite you.

Get prepared for high-vibe energy to show up! **You want you to feel and be the CEO of your own world.**

I used to be the kind of girl who only shopped at TJ Maxx and Marshalls. While I adore this chain of stores and one stop-shopping (scented candles, duvet covers, open-toe sandals and little black dresses all in one place? YES PLEASE!) if I want to create a winning mindset, that also starts with thinking a bit more abundantly. With this, has come with permission to invest a little more on my clothes, and in turn, myself. White House, Black Market is my latest obsession. And while it wasn't easy at first to be comfortable wearing $100 jeans, that one small change made me feel like a million bucks...*and then act like it.*

And ladies, if I'm being really honest, I think the days we feel our best are also the days we put on our sexy pant-ies. You know exactly which ones I'm talking about, I know you do! We all have our good day underwear and our bad day underwear. Let's kick our baggy bad day underwear—the stretched-out ones with holes and period stains—to the curb! Good riddance to ya! My husband would also be thrilled if I tossed these grandma panties!

Let's put our best foot forward by stepping into better clothes choices all around. I am worth it. *I am so worth it.* And those quality jeans and sexy panties remind me of that every time I put them on—I'm worth it.

*Decide that you're worth it too.*

## Confidence Looks Good on You

Let's talk about confidence here for a minute. Confidence comes from you liking the way you look, *not how you think you should look.* So I'm going to get real intimate with you for a second. I've done some things that helped me like ME better: a boob job, eyelash extensions, spray tans, microblading of my eyebrows. Bi-weekly gel manicures are standard practice. Maybe you have had a "mommy makeover" complete with a butt lift and tummy tuck. Maybe you've gotten hair extensions and botox?

Any of these sound familiar? Let's not judge one another! Do you feel better? Did it make you *like you?* Build your confidence up?

*Good! You go girl! YOU DO YOU! Now excuse me while I run to my botox appointment...*

Eighty percent of life is about showing up. Make sure you are showing up for yourself every day. That's not to say you can't dress down the other twenty percent on the weekends or when you're not feeling good. But even if you're not in the mood, I dare you to put on a winning outfit, go get the blowout, pay for those eyelash extensions and do what makes you feel good and confident. Then watch your outside appearance transform your inside attitude.

*What do you need to do differently to show up for yourself?*

*Chapter 4*

## Do Hard Things First

Doing just the easy things will never make you stronger or set you up to win. Just like I could have ridden the bigger waves when I was a little girl at the Jersey Shore that one afternoon. It's important to do hard things and getting them over and done with early in your day is crucial before your mind convinces you otherwise.

Doing the hard things first in your day not only gets them out of the way, but it also builds up the Bank of You. It will give you confidence and will set the pace for the rest of your day. When you do the hard stuff first thing in the day, it doesn't hold up as much mental space. It doesn't take control of you as it would if you let it linger. Do the hard things first and then the rest of the day will flow.

Let's say for example, you had to make a phone call you're dreading because, let's be real, we've all been there. You could wake up and call first thing in the morning during business hours or, you could wait until 2:00 in the afternoon. If you do it first thing in the morning, when your mental focus is on point, you don't have to think about the rest of the day. You get to move on to new things and you don't have to even think about it anymore. You feel accomplished.

So as the saying goes, eat that frog and get the hard things out of the way first. You want to preserve as much brainpower for your good, and by doing those hard things first, you'll be able to do so.

In 2012, my athlete friends convinced me to join them in competing in an Ironman competition. For those of you that don't know, an Ironman is an endurance race that consists of a 2.4-mile swim, a full bike ride of 112 miles, and then 26.2 mile run—a full marathon. It's all back to back within the same day. Totally cray-cray, I know. However, this challenge I was preparing for required me to get after it first thing in the morning—eat one big huge, massive frog six days a week.

I trained for 30 weeks and every morning I would get up at 4 AM before I got my kids ready and then I went to work.

I did this for 30-weeks straight. There was no other way I could have trained for this event if I hadn't done the hard stuff—the swimming, biking and running sessions—in the morning and gotten it done before my day began.

I'm not going to lie, sometimes I woke up and it sucked. It really did. But I did it. And I completed the event. I did more in those two hours in the morning than some people do in their whole entire day. I powered through. I can now proudly say that I've completed five full Ironman competitions. This would not have been possible if I had not done the hard stuff first thing in the morning and just GOTTEN IT DONE.

So whether you're completing an Ironman race or you need to do a project that you've been procrastinating on, do it first thing in the morning while you're fresh, before your brain decides to tell you different.

Because if you wait to do it in the evening, chances are you'll either be too tired or something will come up. There are far too many distractions that can easily throw you off your course if you wait to do what you need to do until later.

Whether you are an early riser or not, you should train yourself to get into the habit of getting the hard stuff done first. Your brain works better when you clear your mental space first and then move on. **It will be hard.**

Your brain won't want to change. It will resist starting a new routine or getting up earlier.

But take small steps and work with yourself rather than against yourself. Eventually, you'll be able to incorporate your new changes.

Getting the hard stuff out of the way first will make more deposits in the Bank of You to build your character. Tackle the difficult tasks head-on at the beginning of each day, and get what you need to do done. Be mentally and emotionally prepared to win by focusing on your most important activities first.

*What tasks do you need to get done first thing in the morning?*

*Chapter 5*

## Learn To Let Go

S tart to let go of a few things to truly start winning your day.

### Take Your Breaks

Information overload is such a real thing. Far too often, I see women sitting at their desks, not taking breaks, and then crashing. These women think they are being productive by doing *all the things,* but really it is a cry for help.

You may think it is helpful to sit eight hours straight at a desk crunching at a computer, but the informed you knows you'll feel much better, and actually get more done, with more breaks.

Breaks don't make you lazy and they shouldn't make you feel guilty. Breaks are so vital and essential to health and overall success.

Like the analogy goes, put your own oxygen mask on first before you go helping others. *Take your breaks.*

The other day I didn't have time to get my reading done during my Sunrise Self Care morning routine. So I put my feet up and plopped down in the middle of the afternoon to read my book. But I just couldn't do it. I started having a little guilt trip.

**I almost felt guilty for pausing in the middle of a busy day to catch up on reading.**

But then I said to myself, "No, you know what? I deserve this. This is my time and I can read right now."

It takes courage to take breaks because our culture tries to make us feel guilty for doing it.

You might have this little silent voice in the back of your head, like I did, telling you it's not right to take a break. Ignore it. Rise above it. And take your breaks anyway.

You'll also need to schedule your breaks or they won't happen. As we learned earlier, our calendar is our boss. Just like you schedule your meetings and kid activities, you have to schedule your breaks. Add them to your calendar when you're going to read for a half-hour or go for a ten-minute walk. It could be as simple as doing a fifteen-minute guided meditation or having coffee with a friend, but schedule breaks on your calendar.

When it's scheduled you're blocking it off and keeping other people from adding things in this time slot. And you're reminding yourself to take the time and do it.

You will come back feeling recharged and refreshed.

Taking breaks also gets you off your electronics for a bit and we could all use a little less screen time. It delivers oxygen to your brain and lungs and makes you tap into your creative juices. It helps you think more clearly and pumps fuel into your body.

Our culture prioritizes productivity and people wear their tiredness and business as a badge of honor by saying terms such as "Team no-sleep", "I'll sleep when I'm dead" or "No days off". If someone tells you they are *so busy*...it really is a red flag that their life is unbalanced. No one should ever be *that* busy.

It is not sexy to talk about the number of breaks you took today, but, I encourage you to fight past the norm and honor rest. Make sure you're taking breaks to show up recharged, centered, and as your best self. It won't be easy, but it will be so worth it. Not just for yourself, but for your family, friends, and community.

As women, we wear many hats and pour our energy out onto so many other people. We are lovers and givers. It's what we do. It's who we are. Taking breaks is not selfish, it's vital for your health. Because if you stop taking your breaks and work all the way through, you will begin to start experiencing burnout. Your body will start failing you. Your mind will become groggy. And you will feel fatigued. Take your breaks.

I used to squeeze in as many zoom meetings and calls as I could in my day, sacrificing the dinner time hour. I would oftentimes get bad digestion having wolfed down my food, not stopping to honor that time with my kids.

One evening, I put my foot down and said "No. I'm done living this way."

So now I sit down and eat dinner in peace. I block out 4 pm-6:30 pm on my schedule every night to sit down and eat dinner mindfully. I take this time also for my adult kids, who have their own busy lives, and do my best to engage with them. I try to make sure I'm available if they need me. If someone tries to worm their way into that time slot? The answer is NO.

When I step away, I can re-engage with a whole new perspective. When I work back to back, I am more impatient, I rush through things, and I am not giving my best self.

## Doing What You Love

Girl, we only have so much time on this earth and we need to stop wasting time on stuff that we just don't love. Believe me, I *want* to be the kind of woman who loves yoga or wants to take up golf. Or someone who enjoys strolling through art museums. Or enjoys gambling or staying at the bar until 1:00 AM (my husband would like this too!). But I'm not and I'm done apologizing for that.

Why is it so hard to be ourselves? To be us? It sounds so simple, and it's a piece of advice people have been doling out for thousands of years. And yet, it's very very hard to do. I've realized one of the reasons is that although you can choose what you do, you can't choose what you *like* to do. You can't control your tastes.

In an effort to win the day, to win at life. I've simply decided to give myself permission to stop doing things that don't truly set my soul on fire. Even if I want to love them. For example, I've been a lifelong reader. But I know ten pages in whether or not I will love a book. I used to force myself to continue reading books because I hate to give up on things. But I've decided I simply no longer want to spend my precious moments doing things I don't immensely enjoy and love.

I'm giving you permission to do the same. Just be you. You do want to challenge yourself to get out of your comfort zone, sample new experiences, and be open to new opportunities. However, if after a time you realize that thing just isn't your jam? Stop immediately. Don't continue. It's okay to let go and move on. Be you because *you are amazing* and the world needs more of who you are and not just who you THINK you should be or what you think you should be doing.

*How can you squeeze in more breaks and let*
*go of things that no longer serve you?*

*Chapter 6*

## Check off your Winning Wowzas!

To win today, you need some Winning-Wowzas. And I have a whole list of them you can check out at www.WinTodayBook.com. Start your day off with a winning list and acknowledging your wins, no matter how small.

**What do you want to accomplish for the day?**

Winning Wowzas are different from your ordinary to-do list. This Winning-Wowza checklist is going to have emotion-packed items on it.

Things like paying your bills and going grocery shopping are also important, but you also need to tap into a list on a deeper level to accomplish the things that make us feel centered, connected, and balanced.

When you wake each morning you should ask yourself what do you want your day to look like? And what can you do to make your day the best day possible? Think of these as a winning list instead of a task list that will leave you feeling just as satisfied as the most perfectly crafted to-do list. These are items that actually have a bit more meaning and will lift your soul and spirit. Here are a few examples:

Call my mom
Schedule coffee with a girlfriend
Try that new skincare routine
Make your manicure appointment
Register for that women's empowerment seminar
Reach out to thank someone
Research that trip and book that Airbnb
Join that walking group
Listen to that podcast

Then go do those things to make it happen. At night, before going to bed, reassess your day and see if you measured up. Did you check off some of these Winning Wowzas? If yes, great, but if not, we get back on the saddle again tomorrow. How are you going to win the next round?

If you notice that a Wowza is reoccurring on your plate because you didn't do it the day before, ask yourself, is this really that important to me? Can I remove it from the list even though I didn't complete it? Re-examine why it's still there. It may not be a "wowza" for you after all.

Winning Wowzas should *feel good*. They should make your heart sing and get you excited just by writing them. Yes, while they may be some "hard things" on there as well and things you know you should do but have been procrastinating on (*Mom, I am so grateful that your name still comes up on my phone*), this list should be chock full of soul-lifting and bucket-filling items.

This is all part of building up your winning reserve.

### Checking Your Energy

When you have to constantly check your gas tank or your bank account to see how much reserves you have left, you're wasting precious mental space.

I remember a time in my life when I had to always check on how much money I had. It was exhausting. I would get stressed out having to calculate my expenses realizing I was just getting by. Whereas now, I can't even tell you when the last time was that I even checked my account because I know I'm good.

Imagine setting yourself up knowing that you will always have enough in your tank or account? Imagine not having to waste mental energy checking to see if "you're good". This is the same approach when fueling your Bank of You. When you make deposits on a daily basis, you're building up your confidence and self-worth.

You never have to worry if you have enough or say, "Oh crap, can I get through this?" You know you have your own back. So by adding to your Winning-Wowzas list and your Bank of You, you're adding a deposit to your energy reserves.

Your focus should be forward. You shouldn't have to always be wondering whether or not you will be okay. You should know at all times that you are all right and you've got your back.

*How will you set yourself up so you know you're covered?*

Chapter 7

## Embrace the Suck

L et's get clear on this babe: *some days are going to suck.* Even when you're doing everything right, things are going to suck, feel hard, and be frustrating for damn sure.

**However, the show must go on.**

Embracing the suck is like childbirth. Whether you eventually get the drugs or not, some part of the experience will be painful. It will hurt. There will be a cramp or two or a hundred. You're going to say the F-word, scream obscenities at your partner and the unphased hospital staff. You will get sweaty and messy and swear you will never be back here again or scream, *"Don't you GET it? I just can't do it!"* (Those poor Labor and Delivery nurses don't get paid enough!)

Like the time I was late to the hospital too far gone to get any drugs, and had to squeeze my beautiful 10 lb. Emma Rose, my third child, out of my *who-ha*. "Nurse...WAIT!!!! I have to go number 2!!!" Ummmm...no. *That would be your daughter's head.* I will spare you the details, but that was an experience, to say the least.

Those of us blessed to be mothers know that childbirth requires a certain kind of grit: your body just takes over and you're able to get through it regardless of how shitty it can be. Can you believe I returned to the hospital to have a fourth child? Knowing the type of pain I endured during my third pregnancy, I came back.

We always need to come back friends, to get up and go again.

Days are going to suck, but we are stronger!

Since we know in advance that there will be hard days, let's prepare for them. Let's be ahead of them, that way when they are here, they don't kick us on our asses, but rather we greet them and take them head-on with a vengeance.

Beautiful things can come from pain. Many of life's lessons will come from the challenging moments in your life. So instead of running from them, embrace them.

When a sucky day greets you, greet it back. Embrace a bit of suffering and get through the hard days. You will have built up a reserve for the next hard day when it comes (Bank of You!) and be less afraid of it, less intimidated by it. It won't impact you as much or shake the faith in yourself. Know that tough times and the "winters" of our life will come and this too shall pass, but we will be better off for going through it.

It's like getting up and going to that Bootcamp class with that really tough instructor and she pulls out that weighted sled or sets up cones for suicide drills. Ugggg!! You start sweating before the first burpee and feel a lump grow in your throat. But you chug your water, keep your head held high, and you muscle through it like a champ anyway.

I was in Hawaii in 2019 competing in another Ironman race and I'll never forget when one of the volunteers asked me from the sidelines, "Why do you do this? Why do you put yourself through this?"

I paused and took a sip of my electrolyte drink. "Because when I'm out there, and I'm on mile 18 of the run after swimming 2.4 miles, biking 112 miles, and I'm just dying, I know it's gonna' suck and I'm going to be suffering. But that's when I come face-to-face with *who I am and what I can really do*." It's when I'm able to push past that pain and get to the finish line that I know what I'm truly capable of.

After every one I say, "I'm never going back, *these just suck!*" But having done five full Ironman races, I guess you could say I always went back for more.

Embracing the suck simply makes you better.

## Positivity is Like a Muscle

Positivity is not always something that comes easily. We tend to be negative by default, it's human nature. I actually think negativity is a defense mechanism for shitty days, to protect ourselves when things ultimately go wrong or don't work out.

Positivity is like a muscle we have to strengthen and build over time. We need to get into the habit of *choosing* to be positive each and every day. Choose it upon waking before your feet hit the floor.

I wasn't always positive. There was a time I used to wake up and dread the day. I would drag into the kitchen and pour the caffeine and well... *crap on the day*. From experience, I can tell you that coffee and complaining are not a winning combination.

Over lunch with a friend one day, she asked me, "Why not do the opposite?" I paused, mid-bite, fork with a dangling lettuce leaf in hand. *What a concept!* What would happen if I just decided to be positive instead? Try it for just one day. Greet the day with gratitude and hope instead of doom and gloom.

Act as if I was approaching the best day ever!

So the next day I tried it and what followed was pretty darn amazing: *I had a good day.* So I did it again the following day. And then the next. As soon as a negative thought popped into my head, I switched it for a positive one. And here is what I noticed: Things went my way! The day flowed easier! I was nicer! People were nicer back!

I found myself calmer, happier, and even felt lighter! I didn't snap at my kids or throw snarky comments at my husband. I even called my mother and she remarked at my changed, upbeat, less tense mood. I then decided to adopt a winning mantra of sorts to say when negative thoughts snuck their way in, which they often did, which was just the old me trying to pull me back into my "safe" cocoon of negativity. Instead, I chose the new and improved ME. I chose me by saying, *"Today I Choose to Win."* and this became my new rallying cry.

> *So, how do you react when your day sucks? How can you change that and choose to be positive?*

## Chapter 8

# Give Into Your Power

### The Power of Next

Give yourself the power of next! If you made a wrong decision or didn't get one of your Winning-Wowzas accomplished? No worries. Because guess what? You have the *power of next.*

Tap into this power and realize it is a gift, my friend. We may make several mistakes during the day, who doesn't? But realizing that we essentially are in control of our lives will make it a little easier.

When working with clients in my health coaching business, we don't have cheat meals or cheat days, *we have choices.* If somebody makes a choice that takes them away from their goals, I say, "That's okay girlfriend, because you have the ***power of next***. It's what you do in the next two or three hours that matters most. So you ate something that didn't take you towards your goal. It's all good because what you do next, that's the secret to success."

Don't let your mistakes overwhelm you. Far too often, people will feel really guilty for their behaviors and mistakes and then let it paralyze them from moving forward. We have to pick ourselves up and let the show go on. Don't get stuck in the sticky parts of life. Remember from the last chapter to embrace the suck and move onward.

*Get in an argument with your husband?* Go say I love you. *Say something you regret to a colleague?* Go apologize. *Say something silly in a staff meeting?* Laugh at yourself. *Snap at your kids unnecessarily?* Go hug them. *Drank an entire bottle of wine when you only meant to have a glass?* Wake up tomorrow and hit that water hard. *Quit halfway through your run?* Go back out there tomorrow and try again.

When things go wrong as they inevitably will, when life *happens*, when you "mess up", it's nothin' but a thing: cause you've got the *power of next* my friend. It's not what you do in the moment, it's what you do next that matters *more.*

Because it's what you do next that will build up your grit factor, strengthen your resilience and make larger deposits in that Bank of You.

We may make mistakes, but we have the power of next to move forward and make better decisions later on. So do not dwell on your mistakes because you have several opportunities awaiting you. Also, it is important to view life from the perspective that new and better things are always blossoming into fruition. Things are always working out for your good and a higher purpose.

When we lean into the power of *next*, it puts ownership back into our own hands. It makes us the leaders of our lives and we get to decide which avenues and territories we're going to journey to next.

## Look for Winning Windows

Look for windows of opportunity and for things that challenge you. Now that you have your Bank of You filled up and your wowzas in check, let's get you even further out of your comfort zone and pump up the volume. What would life be like if you turned it up a notch?

After my last Ironman race in 2019, I finally decided to get my nagging left hip checked as it had been bothering me for the better part of the year, making running extremely difficult. The diagnosis was shocking: I had no cartilage left and was bone on bone. Yikes. Knowing the only option to restore my gait, which had become severely altered, was surgery. The procedure went smoothly, but the recovery was brutal: I couldn't walk without a walker and then cane for weeks, needed physical therapy to sit and stand without assistance and had to retrain myself to walk normally. Humbling experience to say the least.

I couldn't even imagine running again.

Seven months later, I decided it was time to get back to formal exercise and got on the treadmill. At first, all I could do was alternate between walking and running, only for 30 seconds at a time. Boy oh boy, was that frustrating, more mentally than physically.

But it was the window of opportunity I needed to fall in love with running again, which had become more like a chore in recent years. This "reset button" reminded me of why I started running and doing triathlons in the first place, which I had lost sight of, while also forcing me to try new forms of exercise in the interim while healing. This window of opportunity gave me a new perspective.

Looking for winning windows can also challenge us to adopt new skill sets and become more open to opportunities that will help us grow.

I never used to be open to public speaking. It made me uneasy. But I got better at it by looking for *winning windows*. I knew the more I did it, the better I will become. Team Zooms lead to Facebook lives which led to me speaking on stage at a health coach conference, speaking to a group of women prisoners who were looking to rehabilitate themselves (Hey we all have to start somewhere!). And most recently, my very own podcast, "Win Today with M.E.!"

At first? I was terrible. I would trip over my words or talk too fast. But the more I practiced, the more comfortable I was in my delivery. It's these little steps that can lead to big victories. Look for any and all opportunities and winning windows to crack open, just a notch at first. Create space for you to make it happen.

## Envision Yourself Winning

When I envision myself winning, I drill down in my mind to every last detail. I have a big dream of one day *speaking on stage in front of thousands*. SOMEONE has to be the next Mel Robbins….why not ME?

I visualize this dream often. Maybe it's a TED TALK. Maybe it's my own Jersey Girl Win Today conference. Maybe I am speaking at a women's leadership event? *I can see it, taste it, feel it!* I know what I'm wearing and I can see myself surrounded by the people I love most.

I know my husband will be backstage peeking through the curtain and I know the restaurant where we would be going afterward to celebrate. I know I'm going to have a lot of messages on my phone and people are going to be on my social media loving my speech and sharing it. This highlight reel is crystal freaking clear, *every last detail.*

These images are so vivid in my mind. During my Sunrise Self-Care, I spend time seeing it in my mind's eye, bringing it more into focus. It takes practice to be able to see so vividly, but once you get the hang of it, you won't want to stop. For anything big and little in your life, I want you to envision it. It's like creating a mental vision board for yourself.

## Let Your Habits Win Today

On days you don't feel like it, your habits will win the day for you. You might not feel like writing in your journal, or drinking your water, or having a winning mantra. But that's okay.

*Because it's your habits that are going to carry you through when your willpower can't.*

I never used to be big on drinking water. But now, I drink a gallon of water a day. It's almost instinctual and my body craves it. Some days I'm on fire and other days not so much. But because I rely on my habits to guide me through, even on the days when my energy is off, it's not even a question or whether or not I will get in the right amount of hydration. *I just do it.*

It's not that winners are more motivated or inspired, it's that their habits, structure, rituals, and routines are in place and kick in when they are not feeling motivated. Let these last few chapters serve as a launching pad for some new, daily habits to take root in your day. And remember, it's not what you do *sometimes* that produces extraordinary results... it's what you do *consistently that wins today.*

*Stop for a second and envision a grandiose goal or massive dream you have. Visualize every detail. What comes up for you? What do you see?*

**So there you have it dear reader….a blow-by-blow blue-print, a sure-as-shit strategy, a go-get-em guide from this Jersey Girl, your new BFF, to Win Today.**

**Now let's move on to what you need to STOP doing to live your best life.**

# Section 2

## What Jersey Girl Says to Stop Doing

## Chapter 9

# Getting In Your Own Damn Way

### Giving Up On Yourself

When you give up on yourself, it weakens the Bank of You, and it becomes easier and easier to keep quitting.

If you quit every time you start something, it becomes easier to quit every single time things get too hard. People don't give themselves the opportunity to break through and bust through when they hit a wall. We want to make sure in these hard moments to keep going. Living your best life depends on it.

There are things that are gonna happen. Life will get in the way. But you and only you are responsible for your life. *Giving up continuously is also giving up the power to change it.*

When we stay true to commitments we make to ourselves, we set a new standard and increase integrity with ourselves. When we get back up, and we try again, we increase this belief in ourselves, and this creates a winning momentum. There will be so many times on your journey to a new you when you feel like giving up, but keep going! You got this, girl!

## Staying Down When You Fall

We all fall down—mentally, physically, emotionally, professionally and personally. On these days you must rise, you can't stay down. Remember, broken crayons still color. Sometimes bad things need to happen to inspire us to change.

When you fall down seven times, rise eight. Some people are great when things are going well but fall apart when things aren't. Sometimes when bad things happen to us, they are really blessings in disguise. You have to use your mistakes as fuel. Let obstacles become the way. Success is never final, failure is never fatal. It's courage that counts.

How do we find the courage to continue in the face of failure?

I want you to think of yourself as someone who's able to overcome tremendous adversity. As someone who gets up no matter what. Tell yourself that you have what it takes. Remember things happen *for you* and *not to you*.

In 2014, I fell HARD. I was competing in my second Ironman competition in Lake Placid, NY. As if a 140.6 mile endurance event wasn't challenging enough, that day it was thunder and lightning and pouring rain. *Fun times.* The roads were slick for the 112 mile bike portion of the race and I was riding my brakes hard. At mile 40, an athlete from the opposite lane crashed into me head on. We both went spilling over our handlebars and I hit the pavement, sliding into the guardrail. Blood oozed from my left arm and I was disoriented. I quickly got my bearings and realized my bike was intact. So I hopped back on.

***I'm finishing this race damn it!!*** I had trained for 30 weeks and had sacrificed so much. I wasn't going to let this take me down. Grinding it out on a hill a few short miles later, fellow cyclists passing by gave the girl with the road rash and the shoulder wound strange looks. "Hey....do you know your uh...***bleeding?***"

*Nothing to see here. Move right along please.*

I could have easily stayed down and called it quits that day. But I got up and kept going.

Another great example was a few years ago, when I got caught up in a scam on Linkedin. It was one of those deals where they asked you to be a "secret shopper" and buy gift cards for Walgreens, CVS, Rite Aid, and the like. Desperation makes you do some crazy stuff and I needed extra money for Christmas gifts for my children. Long story short, I lost $2,000. *Which was all I had in my bank account at the time.* I couldn't believe it. I was an educated woman with her Master's Degree, yet I let this happen to me. This was such a punch in the gut.

Girlfriends, I had fallen yet again, in a totally different way and one that was actually more devastating. I took to my bed for a week. I was just so defeated, depressed and didn't really know what to do next. *How How How...could I be so stupid?* But talk about obstacles becoming the way: it was during this time that health coaching was offered to me. ***Fine! OK! Yes! I'll do it!*** I agreed reluctantly as a way to simply make up for the lost cash. Little did I know that one little YES was the beginning of something special, a gift that would change the trajectory of my entire life. Ahhhh Universe, you sure know what you are doing!!

Fall, but don't stay down. Use failures to *fuel you forward.*

## Being Satisfied

*Be satisfied with being unsatisfied.*

When you take a bite of something yummy, do you stop there? No! You want more. Let yourself be okay with wanting more. Gritty, resilient people love the chase just as much as the capture. Find beauty in the journey and the pursuit! Be blessed, but not satisfied. It is A-okay to want more from this one life we get to live.

Be hungry, want more from your life and know you were meant for more. You should always strive to want to be better, to do better, to get better.

Let's look at Tom Brady as an example. *Side note: I am barely qualified to make a football reference here, but try to stay with me.* He could have easily been satisfied with his time with the New England Patriots, retired, and left the league. He still would have been called the G.O.A.T. (Greatest Of All Time!) but he didn't retire. He wanted MORE.

Truth be told, he's probably training just as hard today as he did when he started, if not harder. But winners stay hungry for more and when they accomplish one goal, they immediately set another, never satisfied.

I had achieved a pretty significant milestone in my coaching business fairly early on. It was a goal I had set for myself and I went on for it! My mentor remarked soon after,

"Well, you've hit the mark. There's nothing next!" I thought to myself, *"There's nothing next? Come AGAIN?"* So much is NEXT. *In fact, this is just the beginning!* Am I going to stop helping people? There are so many others on my team who have yet to reach their goals. There are so many other lives I can transform. There are so many others who need meaningful change in their lives. There are so many other ways I can inspire and lead, including writing this book*! You're welcome!*

For me, there is no finish line. The destination just keeps changing as I set new goals and challenges for myself that push me out of comfort zones and into continued growth. I pivot and shift to embrace new chapters of my life, and rise up to the role those require of me. In our quest to pursue our best selves, we need to be uncomfortable with being comfortable. Stay hungry babe.

### Avoiding That ONE Thing

Are you delaying something you know you should be doing?

Is it finally getting healthy or switching jobs? Having that hard conversation? Walking away from a difficult friendship or planning lunch with friends you haven't seen in a while?

*I guarantee you that ONE thing you are avoiding? Will help you grow, girlfriend. Or will set you free.* That ONE thing, in a nutshell, is holding you back.

These ONE things, those pesky little suckers, get moved to the back burner when it comes to acting on them. By making them a much bigger deal than they need to be, they are stealing your energy and power. Get clear on what that is for you and stop putting it on delay.

Do you want to know the one thing I kept putting off that drove me insane? It was hopping on the scale and looking at what the numbers revealed to me. Crazy, I know! I get the irony of this ya'll...being a Health Coach and all! Insert eye roll here....

But I couldn't do it. I wouldn't do it.

As a recovering perfectionist, seeing those numbers gained a ridiculous hold on me. Regardless of how I looked in the mirror or felt in clothes, the numbers never lied and had the power to make or break me, depending on the day.

At the doctor's office, I would look the other way or close my eyes. *"Nurse...would you mind if I stood backward and upside down? I'm sure you get this all the time..."*

It became a huge burden in my life because I didn't know how much I weighed. This stopped me from doing a bunch of other activities in my life because I was so focused on my weight.

Recognizing I was a fraud of a Health Coach if I didn't come face-to-face with this demon, I knew it was something I had to overcome. Structural tension is a beautiful thing, and it was exactly what I needed to get over my fear of the metal monster. *Band-aid ripped. Wounds exposed. Freedom achieved. Avoidance no more.*

Facing the ONE thing you have been avoiding and dreading, that thing that scares you most, is another deposit you will be making into the Bank of You to build up your credibility with yourself.

**The best time to take action is now.**

Sometimes we may feel tired, lazy or maybe the task at hand is difficult to complete so we think the best solution is to do it later. A lot of the time later turns into never.

The biggest lie you will ever tell yourself is that you will do it in five more minutes. Nope! It's best to get it done NOW. *1-2-3 - GO GIRL!* Learning to face and deal with the thing you are avoiding will set you free to move forward and win in any area of your life.

What are you avoiding?

## Telling Yourself Stories

It's not who you are that's holding you back...it's who you *think* you're not.

Are you playing the same narrative, movie, or story in your head and sticking to it? Are you clinging to a former identity?

When you give the stories in your head power, you stay the victim instead of being the dominant force in your own life. When you label yourself with an old identity, that may have been you back then, but that is not who you are now. Begin to let go of old identities of who you thought you should be and start to tell yourself a different story, you hold the pen and begin to write a new one.

My husband used to always tell me he wasn't the brightest bulb in the batch. He comes from an entrepreneurial, plumbing family and, a teacher said to him one day, *"You're just going to thread pipes for a living."* That type of shit can run long and deep in your subconscious mind. *Teacher friends, you have no idea just how powerful your words can be!* Anytime he was challenged to do something intellectually, he would fall back on that old narrative and it became a deep-rooted, limiting belief. I said, "Don't let this story identify who you are as a person. Challenge that script!"

So he decided to turn on a *new* lightbulb in his head, flip the script and told himself a new truth. And guess what? My man immerses himself in personal development and runs towards growth and learning opportunities every chance he gets. He now begins every day reading, spends his free time listening to podcasts and attends seminars and workshops to level up in his life whenever he can. He decided to tell himself a different story.

So what are the certain narratives you're telling yourself? Do you see these limiting beliefs holding you back? Some might say:

> "Well, I'm a mother who needs to be home for her kids. I can't start that side business right now."

> "I'm not a morning person."

> "I am just not financially savvy."

> "I'm just not lovable. I'll never find the perfect partner".

> "I would love to run, but I'm just not the runner-type."

> "Oh, I've always been the funny, fat friend. I can't be the thin, sexy person who's wearing cool clothes."

"Oh, I'm a foodie. I really can't lose weight and give up drinking because I just love food".

It's almost like a defense mechanism for lacking an ability to change. You have to be willing to let go of who you think you are and become who you're truly meant to be.

When your mind starts playing that movie, quickly swap it out for a new highlight reel. Think of a time when you were happy, or a photo of you smiling, doing what you love. Use that as a "commercial" that interrupts your show.

*What's an old limiting belief you can let go of?*

*Chapter 10*

## Holding Yourself Back

### Letting Your Inner Critic Have the Floor

Thoughts become things. Be careful how you talk to yourself.

Do you find yourself saying things like: "I am a hot mess. I am the worst. I wish I looked like him or her. I feel fat. I'm not the sharpest tool in the shed."

Self-deprecating thoughts are powerful and they will suck the life out of you. Become aware of them as they will try to keep you stuck and tell you you're not good enough, pretty enough, thin enough, smart enough, brave enough.

Most of the time, our thoughts are on autopilot. Our subconscious brain is constantly telling us one thing or another. Take control of them and stop giving them power.

Start switching out negative words for positive ones and take your power back!

Many of the health coaches I work with are women, who have spent a lifetime putting themselves down and enclosing themselves in a cloud of negativity. They have to put in consistent effort to let those old mindsets go. When I see someone struggling in their business, phrases like, "I can't keep a client!" or, "I have another quitter today!" are often part of our conversations. Despite stumbles and hiccups, I challenge them to focus on the positive, to write and to speak about the things *that are going well for them.* Trust me, friends, there are always things positive to be found. When we frame words and thoughts differently, we can train our brains to switch up our thinking from negative to positive.

If I'm being completely transparent with you, taking the courage to even write this book has been challenging for me.

My inner critic told me at times, *"Mary Ellen, you can't do this."* Or, *"Who am I to write a book?"* Limiting beliefs like, *"Oh maybe it's just not the right time to write a book,"* have popped into my head all throughout this process.

Thoughts like, *"Do I even know enough?"* or *"Am I ready?"* have circled through my mind. Believe me, babe, you will never feel ready. For anything. *Ever.* If you wait for the timing to be right when you no longer have doubt or question marks, you will never do anything great in your life. Those goals and dreams you put on paper will simply stay there.

The quickest way to silence your inner critic is to embrace the uncertainty and use that fear as fuel to move you forward...*and take action.* In fact, when I have trepidation about doing something? It's like a neon sign blinding me on the highway of progress to say *YES! DO IT! NOW!* Action makes you brave.

I now use my inner critic to direct me out of my comfort zone and towards opportunities and risks that are important for my growth. *And thank God I do, or else you would not be reading through these pages at this very moment.* Use self-doubt and sabotaging thoughts as motivation to move.

## Giving Away Your Power

You have the power inside of you. You already have what it takes to win today. So stop giving that power away so damn easily.

You might say something so smart, but then apologize for something so little after speaking so boldly.

For example, if I get on a Facebook Live and say, "I'm sorry if I look like a hot mess, but I have a great message to deliver," then I just gave away all my power. Or "I don't care if people are judging me right now…" that gives a signal that I actually *do care* what others think.

We need to stop doing this! We may think it's cute or makes someone else feel better. But it's watering down our pizazz!!

## Trying to be Perfect

Are you paralyzed by perfectionism? Does your winning streak stop or your focus drop because you start thinking negative thoughts and worrying about what could go wrong? Do you find yourself saying things like: *"What if I'm not good enough?" "I don't know everything yet." "How can I win if I keep messing up?"*

If so, you may be a perfectionist. It's not uncommon considering how our society throws unparalleled demands at us left and right. I'm here to tell you, it's okay to let it go. Let it all go babe.

**Screw being perfect.**

If you make a mistake, call it a creative encounter and embrace it. It takes more energy trying to be perfect than believing things can go right. Remember, you have *the power of next anyway!*

Let's worry about actions, not outcomes.

Don't be attached to the outcome of your work. Whatever happens, happens. When you focus your energy on the actions and have a mental shift, your energy will be in a much more positive place than a constricted and confined area. What if you knew the thing you're working on was going to completely change your life?

How productive would you feel then?

Would you feel motivated to try harder because you knew it was going to work out? You're not thinking about failing or what the outcome is, you just know you're going to succeed. How magical would that be?

If you're feeling stuck because you're worried about being perfect, remember this: ***imperfect action is better than no action.***

Embrace progress each day, not perfection!

Also, trying to be perfect all of the time kills creativity. Imagine all the things that won't get accomplished because you wanted them to be perfect. Sometimes, you just have to let loose and go with the flow.

Embrace the progress each day, not perfection. Keep going like there's no chance of failure and believe everything will work out. Do the work and take the action. Creating a winning mindset is all about taking daily steps forward versus worrying about being perfect.

In our health coaching business, we ask our coaches to go live on Facebook or Instagram and most of these women are paralyzed with fear of being perfect. They are so worried about what to say, and are afraid of what others may think. I tell them to stop overthinking it, be their authentic selves, speak from their hearts and they won't go wrong. I remind them, "People don't want perfect. They just want *you*. Most people will think you're brave and inspiring. And those who don't? *Well, those are not your people.* Move on."

Get focused on making simple progress each day. Get out of your own head, stop overdramatizing the situation, and screw being perfect.

*What perfect habit can you let go of and let loose from?*

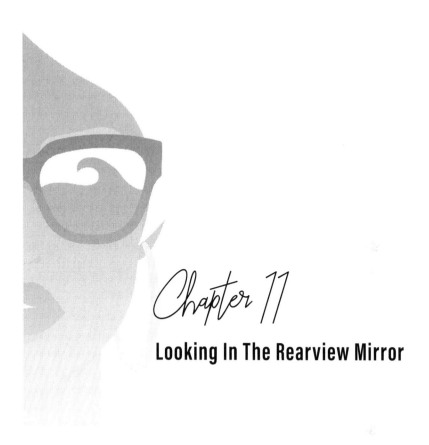

## *Chapter 11*

## Looking In The Rearview Mirror

### Don't Let Your Past Run You Off the Road !

When you think about it, there is a reason why your rearview mirror is so small and the front windshield is a lot bigger. It's because you're not meant to look out the rearview mirror.

You're only meant to be looking forward and occasionally, from time to time, should be looking backward, but only if really necessary. Don't let your past run you right off of the road.

So many times people will let old experiences or hurts hinder them from propelling forward. We've got to stop doing this. You have to focus on your present because the only thing you really have control of is the here and now.

I love this quote from Nelson Mandela, *"I never lose. I either win or learn."*

So whatever happens, as long as we can learn from it and grow from it, that means we can learn something from our past, even if it's small.

We have to make the shift from *"Why did this happen to me?"* to *"What is this trying to teach me?"* There's a reason why the rearview mirror is 100 times smaller than the windshield. It's okay to shift and look forward and use these past experiences as learning lessons. They happened, we can't change it, but we can learn from them. And it's not the actual experiences in your past that are plaguing you. But it's the feelings that are associated with them. *"He broke my heart. I feel like a loser." "They fired me. I'm not hireable."* It's not so much what happened to us, but the feelings we take away from the incidents or experiences that are preventing us from looking ahead and moving forward.

When growing up, I so desperately wanted to be a cheerleader. Who didn't? My two best friends were these cute little cheerleaders types, making posters for the players, wearing adorable little outfits, and getting the attention of the boys. And every girl wanted to be like them. I was no exception. But try as I did, I could barely even hold my fingers together for a normal clapping motion, nor could I do an actual cartwheel or stunt of any kind.

After shockingly not making the cheer roster one year, I actually had my poor mother call the coaches (who literally were only a year or two older than I was) to make sure there was no mistake in the judging. I know...*I'm cringing enough for the both of us.*

**Things happen for you and not to you...**

I just wasn't cut out to be on the sidelines and found myself better suited to be on the field and in the game. It wasn't until I found volleyball in high school and was made the team captain that I discovered my love of team camaraderie and leadership.

I could have kept looking behind and fixating on not making the cheerleading squad, but instead chose to look forward and in doing so, was given some of my greatest childhood memories.

Looking forward doesn't mean you never look back. It just means you are laser-focused, continuing on a clear path, and you refuse to let old junk weigh you down. You refuse to be bombarded by hiccups or roadblocks that occurred.

And since we are now close pals I can share some pretty intimate stuff that's still very raw and real to me: the failure of my first marriage—a "rearview mirror moment" that comes up for me from time to time. What if we stayed together? Who would I be right now? Where would I be now? What would my life look like? Would I be writing this? Would I be the CEO of my own business? So many questions and never any real answers.

But what I do know for certain is this: I love my current husband to death. He is my soulmate and I'm so glad I found him. We've done amazing things together both personally and professionally. He's the reason I'm operating at the frequency I am today.

And I'm so thankful for that. But, I used to beat myself up about my old marriage and said things like, *"Maybe it's me. Mary Ellen, what if you had just tried a little harder?"* I tormented myself about this for years, but it got me nowhere.

After much reflection and thousands of dollars in therapy, I have come to this conclusion: *I needed the old me to die in order for the new me to emerge.* Do you remember that funeral I gave myself where I went out with the old and in with the new version of myself? Well, I mentally and metaphorically ran myself over with a car. I didn't even look out the front windshield first!

Unfortunately, there were many casualties as a result of my decision and I live with that burden every day. At the time, many people in my life called me selfish and bitter. *"Mary Ellen, do you even know what you're doing?"*

No, I didn't. But, it didn't matter. I was following my intuition. I was tuning into the still voice inside of me and going with my gut. Ladies, your gut never lies. Believe her when she speaks up.

Walking away from the life I knew and completely into a new one, was scary as hell. I didn't know at the time if it was the right decision. I just put one foot in front of the other, and propelled myself forward with constant action rather than checking the rearview mirror.

While on this topic, I think it's safe for me to say here, whoever painted the picture of blended families being full of roses and rainbows is full of bullcrap. They lied!

**They are hard, difficult, and can be messy.**

My grown children have navigated a great deal and I know it hasn't been easy for them.

There was one point where I used to make Facebook posts of us all being together as one big happy family, but now, I'm like nope—that's total bullshit!

I don't send out a Christmas card anymore either. It's not that I don't love our family, I do. Our blended family is wonderful and I wouldn't trade it for the world, but I'm no longer sending out the message that we are this perfect family, because we're not.

We do the best we can do and we don't apologize for it. My ex-husband is a great guy, a great father and we are good friends raising four amazing humans together. I couldn't ask for anything more.

Walking away from the old me and giving birth to the new me was part of an awakening. Deciding whether I was going to stay stuck or risk it all to move forward and do the things I felt I was being called towards. And yes, in the wake of that there was heartbreak, a broken family, and residual impact now just emerging 10 years later.

However, I have made peace with my past and have come to terms with what was and what is. Having a growth mind-set, when reflecting on this time, I ask myself, *"What did I learn from this?"* The answers I come up with I have taken into my current marriage and are what make it so strong.

Woulda-Coulda-Shoulda will do you no good. So go live a life of no regrets.

You have to stay in the here and now. You have to trust your decision and know that ultimately, everything will work out. Everything will be okay. So clear your windshield to stay more focused on what's ahead rather than what's behind. Cause you're not going that way.

*What is one thing you can focus on right
now that is in your windshield (Present) and
not your rearview mirror (Past)?*

*Chapter 12*

## Draining Your Bucket

### People Who Don't Want You to Win

The company you keep does have an impact and influence on your choices and your attitudes. They say you become like the five people you spend the most time with. Choose carefully. So, who are you surrounding yourself with? Are they the kinds of people you should be around in order to win? Spending time with like-minded people who have similar goals, attitudes and behaviors will elevate you. So become aware of the company you keep.

Pay very close attention to who claps for you when you win. Unfortunately, there may be close family members and friends who don't share your joy.

Girl, when you are setting a new course and making changes, expect some raised eyebrows, judgement, disapproval and negativity. *Your growth scares them.*

But this has nothing to do with you and everything to do with them. Your leveling up in life turns the mirror on their inadequacies and inability to change. Sometimes, we need to outgrow people to win. To leave someone behind. It's not easy, but it's important.

I'll give you an example. I'm really proud of the business I'm building. It's something I never thought I could do. I mean, not to toot my own horn, but I've been able to pay for my kitchen renovation in cash, pay off credit card debt, travel whenever we can and have money saved up in the bank. I'm at a pretty comfortable place right now.

**You'd think I'd get a "You Go Girl" from time to time from those closest to me.**

*Cricket...cricket...*

Silence speaks volumes. Pay close attention to it. When people see other people making their dreams come true, it's a harsh reality check. Their subconscious mind is telling them, "If they can do it, then why not me too?" This should be a positive thing, but to some, it's a negative.

But that's okay. *Love them anyway.*

While I am still me in so many ways, I have also changed in more ways I can count. Some people still want me to be the old Mary Ellen. The Mary Ellen I was in my old marriage. The Mary Ellen I was in my nine-to-five job. The girl who always played it safe. The one who just did triathlons. The one they're comfortable with. They don't know what to do with this Mary Ellen, but I've learned to let it go.

It's okay to outgrow old behaviors, friends, and communities. It can be hard for women especially because we don't want to come across as a pompous asshole who feels she's too big for her little community. Trust me, I get it.

But now I want to surround myself with people I aspire to be like. I want to surround myself with people who take risks, challenge themselves, level up in life, follow their passions and dreams, make shit happen, and who dare to step outside their comfort zones. I want to step into the game with those who are done playing small and safe. I want to be a part of the dream builders, not the dream stealers.

Go get around the ones who support your goals, lift you up and inspire you to be better. *Go find your tribe and love them hard.*

## Stop Feeding Your Body and Mind with Crap

What are you feeding your body? Your mind? Are you feeding your body and mind in a way that energizes you? Fuels you properly? Or nourishes your soul and spirit?

I'm not just talking about food and water. I'm talking about what you read, and the friends you hang out with. How about the organizations you join or the music you listen to? Or better yet, the television shows you watch or the Netflix binging that consumes you?

All of this makes up part of your psyche and plays a factor in creating a winning mindset.

What about your social media? Who are you following? What are you consuming? Are they motivating you or are they poisoning you?

**You decide!**

Speaking of fueling our bodies, let me tell you about something crazy I used to do.

I used to exercise like a mad woman, eating grilled chicken and green beans perfectly proportioned out in tupperware containers. I did really well sticking to "the plan" and "being good" Sunday through Monday. But when Saturday came around, I had a *cheat meal*. When I say cheat meal, I mean I *really* had a cheat meal. I went all out, and stuffed myself with all kinds of crap. Drinks, appetizers, desserts, you name it. Like a prisoner having his last meal on death row.

Every Saturday, I spent hours picking out the perfect restaurant, and if my meal wasn't just right, we would go somewhere else. I would eat up until the final hour before bed, literally making myself so sick and bloated, I would have to lay on my side all night. Here's the kicker: I probably consumed more calories in that one meal than I had all week, cancelling out the whole week's worth of work. As a result, I didn't even make any changes in my physical appearance and actually gained weight during this time.

*Ay caramba!*

Around this particularly disturbing "cheat meal chapter," I also became obsessed with bodybuilding. I spent my days following female competitors on Instagram, researching various training protocols and coaches, watching competitions at random hotels throughout the tri-state area on weekends. And if you are not judging me enough at this point, *I even went so far as to get breast implants in preparation for my inaugural debut in the master's figure division.* Which, if I may add, *never actually happened.*

*Yeah, that one hurt deep in my core to write.*

To say it became an unhealthy fixation was an understatement.

It really fueled negative energy inside me. Not only did I fuck up my mind, I screwed up my metabolism so badly it took an entire year to feel normal again. And the worst part? *I don't even really know why I wanted to do it? I had no WHY.*

On the verge of a mental breakdown and to the elation of my ever-patient husband, I quit cold turkey. Stopped following the people and stopped going to the gym. I was done feeding both my body and mind with utter crap. It was a few short years later that I found my current health program and it not only taught me how to feed and fuel my body properly, it freed my mind from the prison I was in regarding food and exercise. My health program, which I now share with thousands of others, helped me love myself, maybe for the first time ever. *It saved my life.*

Pay close attention to what we're feeding our bodies and what we're feeding our minds both physically and metaphorically. Does it fuel you to win? Make you feel good about yourself? Lift you up? If the answer is no, just stop. CTRL. ALT. DELETE.

## Stop Comparing Yourself to Others

Just because you're doing things differently doesn't mean you're doing it wrong. There is no time limit to winning.

You have to be like a horse with blinders on. Stay in your own lane. Go at your own pace. So many times we let other people get into our heads and this shifts us off course. Don't let it.

For example, there are leaders in my organization who have larger businesses than I do. Making way more income than me. Escaping to their beach houses in Maui and renting private yachts and jets. I could let it get to me and feel bad because I'm not there yet, or I could use it as motivation to raise my game. I choose the latter.

When we follow people on social media, there are a lot of comparisons that happen. Sometimes that doesn't move us forward, it sets us backward.

Just recently, I got my breast implants removed. They do not serve me anymore. As we now know, I had gotten them at a time that I was fueling my mind in a destructive way, one that harmed me, not helped me. Truth be told, I let the comparison game get to me.

I now feel more free and back to my normal self. As I feel strongly about letting my failures and setbacks be learning lessons for others, I recently shared my experience on social media. The outpouring of support and the private messages I received about women considering similar options validated all of it.

Comparison is the thief of joy. Know that your journey will never be the same as anyone else's and that's okay. Embrace your path.

*What are some things you really love about yourself? Some things you forgot to even look at or pay attention to because you may have been so focused on comparing yourself to others? Focus on what you love about yourself.*

Chapter 13

## Staying Comfortable

G rowth is uncomfortable.

You have to push yourself past your comfort zone. Pain is uncomfortable. But nothing is as painful as staying stuck somewhere you don't belong.

There's a woman inside all of us and she's called: *Comfort Connie.* She wants to keep you on the sidelines. Comfort Connie wants to keep you safe and hold you back. She wants to keep you secure and in the familiar.

Personally, I have to fight Comfort Connie off every single day and say, *"I'm going to do hard things today, Connie, if you want to try to stop me, you're going to be in for a fight."*

You have to be willing to not let Comfort Connie have the floor. Pay attention when she starts to creep in through old habits or tendencies. She doesn't want you to grow or change.

*Comfort Connie...you have other plans.*

The first job I ever had, was as a writer-producer with a video production company. One of our clients was an author who had created a picture book about bridges. He wanted to be interviewed on top of the Brooklyn Bridge. The producer who was supposed to do the interview that day called in sick, so they asked me to fill in. I was just out of college, as green as green could be, *and terrified of heights.* And oh goodie, on that particular day, I happened to be wearing a business suit, shoulder pads and all, *with a wedge heel.* There was no time to change.

Gulp.

In a blur, I was hooked onto these cables and thrust onto the base of one of the bridge's large steel cable lines. *Seriously terrifying.* Inch by inch, I walked up that cable, camera crew in tow, sweating profusely, refusing to look down. One wedge heel in front of the other, I made it to the top and to the interview. The author, cool as a cucumber, was waiting at the top. I will never forget the words he said to me. **"You made it,"** he said.

Yup, that I did.

Every time I see the Brooklyn Bridge, I think about my ability to get *uncomfortable* that day. Lack of comfort provides opportunities for growth and change. If you want to get something in your life that you never had before, you have to do something that you've never done before. *Be ok with being uncomfortable.*

## Don't Stop Dreaming

Remember when you were a kid and you were fearless in your dreaming?

What happened to that? Children dream without reservation. Adults, dream with limitations.

When you were a child, you probably came home from school with many stories and your imagination ran wild.

You have to hold on to your inner child and never stop dreaming.

Think about the health goals you want to reach, the vacations you want to take, the relationships you want to foster, and the business(es) you want to grow. Don't stop dreaming. If someone tells you you can't have something or can't do something, challenge them.

Step out of your comfort zone, stack your wins, embrace the suck, tap into your Bank of You and go after it with all you've got. We can dream again! In order to get where you've always imagined, you must trust and keep going.

Think about the price you'll pay if you stop following your dreams. Is the price more or less than if you stayed where you are?

The lack of sacrifice in your life is code for: *My dream isn't worth fighting for.* When you aren't sacrificing or suffering it means you're not living your life to full potential. Everything worth having isn't easy. And your dream is worth *the hard*. Go work your tail off for it.

Keep pushing towards dreams even though they may seem out of sight. You don't want to leave this earth and die full of dreams, you want to be completely empty, having left a legacy. Anything is possible, so dream big. You do have what it takes to make them your reality.

*What's a big dream you have that you can't stop thinking about? You should probably go do it.*

*Chapter 14*

# Playing the Victim

## Following the Crowd?

All our lives we're told we should be a part of the in-crowd. From the time we're in preschool to the time we hit high school, and then the real world, we look for what is in and veer towards that. I guess you can say it's also a part of our human design.

Our instincts tell us to run the same direction as the crowd rather than the path less taken. You may have reached this at some point in your life and then found that you've wandered off course to the true you. Be courageous enough to recognize it and be courageous enough to blaze your own trail.

Let go of any expectations you think you must meet. Let go of the rules you learned from school and society. Let go of what your girlfriends are doing. Let go of what your mother thinks you should do. Carve your own path.

It'll be scary at times, no doubt, but it will also be worth it. When you start living for yourself, the unimaginable will start happening. You'll feel in control of your life rather than life taking you down. It's an amazing feeling.

Do a self-audit. Are you really living life on your own terms for *you* right now, or are you following the crowd?

## Making Excuses

Are you blaming your past experiences, or other people, places, and things for your lack of success or getting what you want? Learn to be the dominant force in your own life and stop playing the victim card. It's so easy to put the blame onto something else.

Examples:

> *"I can't lose those fifteen pounds because I've hit age 40, and you know our metabolism changes the older we get."*

*"I can't start my business because I'm just not tech-savvy."*

*"I can't write a book because I'm not that well versed."*

*"I can't do (fill in the blank) because I just don't have the time.*

**No, I call bullshit.**

Simply put, it's not that you can't. *It's that you won't.* You aren't willing to make that excuse *a priority* in your life. It's just not that important. When this happens, a victim mentality takes over and we give up all power to be in control of our own lives.

***If it is important to you, you will find a way. If not, you'll find an excuse.***—Ryan Blair

Promise me you will no longer make any excuses that may take you off your path to win the day. You might not even notice them at first because they creep in at a subconscious level. It's a safety net to make you feel good about yourself.

Defense mechanisms occur all the time to make you feel better, but they mask over the real problem causing you not to get the results you want.

So pay attention to any subliminal messages that come your way that sound like protection, but are really just excuses in disguise. Decide right now to take full responsibility for your own life, despite all current circumstances and past experiences. No one is in control of your life but you and you have the power to change anything about it.

Choose excuses. Or chose progress. But you can't have your cake and eat it too.

*In what areas of your life are you playing the victim? What are making excuses about?*

# *Conclusion*

## Scar Up Baby

I have four scars on my body: on my chest from "sweat chafing" of a triathlon suit zipper, on my left shoulder from my bike crash, on my left hip from my hip surgery and underneath my "ta-tas" from my breast implant removal.

I wear each of them like a badge of honor.

Each scar is a reminder of a time in my life when I was brave and courageous, was challenged and uncomfortable, had fallen but got back up, had failed but tried again, and let something that didn't serve me go.

They are a roadmap of my journey and represent a life not lived on the sidelines, but fought hard in the battle, having emerged victorious. *A winner.*

Maybe you have some scars too. Maybe yours are internal and can't be seen. But no matter the type, they symbolize a life worth fighting for. So "scar up baby," cause we are building winners today. And you are worth the fight my friend.

———❦———

*Now you have it, a Jersey Girl's Guide on how to Win Today.*

Just like the tide, our life ebbs and flows, with so many ups and downs, sometimes taking you under, tossing you about, and leaving you gasping for air. After reading these pages, my hope is that you now have a better sense of how to keep your head above water and ride those waves to win.

*And today is a new day to choose to win.*

So let me ask you some simple questions:

*Have you planned that funeral for your old self?*

*Are you excited to walk away from the old you?*

*Are you ready to get out of your own damn way and off the sidelines of your life?*

*Are you ready to stop being so scared and put YOUR dreams front and center?*

*Are you ready to give birth to the NEW YOU, the one who now has the blueprint in her hands to step into the BEST version of herself?*

*Do YOU hear that whisper, that voice, that roar that you were meant for "more"?*

You need to believe right now that you, yes you, are destined to do something magical with your life, that you don't have to settle for your current reality or what others expect of you. I want you to really listen to that whisper, as faint as it may be, and don't dismiss it. Let it speak to you, guide you, nudge you. Embrace it.

By not listening to it, by holding back, playing small and staying on the sidelines, you are robbing yourself of the life of your dreams while robbing us all from your wonderful, authentic self and who you were meant to be.

Remember, it all begins with taking small steps forward each and every day, focusing on actions, not outcomes.

Acknowledging, celebrating and stacking each "win" no matter how insignificant or small they seem. Small steps don't have to mean small thoughts. Build up that confidence and belief in yourself, make deposits in that Bank of You, check off those Winning Wowzas that fill you up and set that winning wave in motion. Again, you can check out some awesome Winning Wowzas at www.WinTodayBook.com.

I want you to pause here and close your eyes. See your winning life in your mind, every single, minute detail. See it. Taste It. Feel it. Dream as BIG as you can. Can you envision it? Now open your eyes.

*Today, I want you to CHOOSE YOU and make a decision that you will move towards that dream, as big and audacious and as scary as it is, and begin to WIN, no matter what.* You had everything you needed before picking up this book, but let these words strengthen what's already inside you. Your dreams are worth going for. YOU are worth fighting for. So go answer that voice that's calling you towards "more".

Now swim out deep and go catch that winning wave babe...and remember to enjoy the ride!

***Let's Win Today!***

# Acknowledgements

*"Alone we can do so little; together we can do so much."*
*Helen Keller*

*E*verything I have done in my life was because someone believed in me before I believed in myself.

To my parents. Everything I am today is because you believed in me first. I may not have traveled the path that you wanted for me, but thank you for loving me anyway. To my mom, my love of books, writing and being open and teachable is all due to you. What a gift you have given me! To my dad: yes...I always listened to that song "Just The Two of Us" when you sang it to me in the car. I just didn't want to admit it to you. :) You know I was born to lead before I did. Thank you for always reminding me of that.

*To my four incredible children, Brendan, Julia, Emma and Harry: In your own quiet way, you let me be me. You have endured, shouldered, and put up with so much and sometimes my heart aches with the love I have for each of you. No matter where I go or what I do in this life, being your mom is the greatest title I will ever have. It has been an absolute privilege to see you grow into the outstanding human beings you have become. Each of you is destined to do something amazing with your life and to make an impact on this world. It has been an honor to give you that start. Go find your happiness, your passion and your purpose. It's waiting for you.*

*To my HealthyMe&You Team: the courage to even start this book was born through your belief in me. It helped me step outside of my comfort zone and put pen to paper. Every success I have as an entrepreneur is because of our team effort. Thank you for empowering me to follow my dreams and set new goals. I bow to you and love you all fiercely. Special thanks to my "advisory counsel" Christeen and Cindy for letting me blow off steam when I needed to without judgement.*

*To my longtime BFF Cathy. You always knew I would write a book someday. Just make sure you are reading this one on the beaches of LBI with a G&T in your hands. Love you Theo. xo*

*To my family. May one day you feel as proud of me as complete strangers are. Until then, I love you.*

*To Suzy Heyman who said...YES...you ARE ready to write a book now. Thanks for nudging my potential girl!!! To my work* husband and "Yoda", Bob Ford, thanks for seeing my future before I could.

To every coach and mentor I've had in this life, from my Dad, to my early swim coaches and recently to Coach Michael Burt... thank you for activating and awakening my prey drive. Everyone needs a coach in life!

And finally to my amazing husband Wayne. Everyone should be loved the way you love me and I am beyond blessed to wake up next to you each morning. You have always known I was meant for "more" and challenged me to move towards it. Your unending and unrelenting support is why we are here today and none of it happens without you. We have seen rock bottom and together fought, crawled and scratched our way to the surface. We are finally seeing the light of day babe and our future looks so bright and dreams are all coming true!! Together, there is nothing we can't do!! YOU&ME!!!! WE GOT THIS!!!! And to our Sargie... thank you for rescuing us and being our one baby together.

To you, my dear reader. Thank you for taking this journey together and for giving my words your time and attention today. What an amazing feeling that is!! Please know that I see you. Let me believe in YOU now before you do. I know you have something great inside of you, and have a unique gift to share with this world. Don't deprive us of that—go share it. Simply begin by winning just today.

# About the Author

*M*ary Ellen Loranger is a Jersey girl who started playing small but now dreams big. A Transformational Coach, she has found her true calling by helping others create meaningful change in their lives, from bodies and minds to careers and finances. When she is not writing her next book, Mary Ellen can be found on Zoom with her Healthy Me&You Team, inspiring others on Facebook Lives, recording her podcast, reading in her big white chair, drinking *coffee overlooking her lake, running on her treadmill or strolling through Central Park with her husband and German Shepard mix Sarge.*

*Learn more at wintoday-me.com.*

Disclaimer: OPTAVIA makes no guarantee of financial success. Success with OPTAVIA results from successful sales efforts, which require hard work, diligence, skill, persistence, competence, and leadership. Please see the OPTAVIA Income Disclosure Statement (bit.ly/idsOPTAVIA) for statistics on actual earnings of Coaches.

Made in the USA
Middletown, DE
01 December 2021